Algrove Publishing Limited
36 Mill Street, P.O. Box 1238
Almonte, Ontario, Canada K0A 1A0

Telephone: (613) 256-0350
Fax: (613) 256-0360
Email: sales@algrove.com

Acknowledgements
*We are grateful to the staff of the **Museum of the Horse Soldier** in Tucson, Arizona for photographs of their uniform collection that made our cover design possible. For interested readers, the museum is at 6541 East Tanque Verde Road in Tucson.*

Library and Archives Canada Cataloguing in Publication

Williams, J. R. (James Robert), 1888-1957
    U.S. Cavalry cartoons / J.R. Williams.

(Classic reprint series)
ISBN 1-897030-16-9

    1. American wit and humor, Pictorial. 2. United States.
Army--Cavalry--Caricatures and cartoons. I. Title. II. Series: Classic reprint series
(Almonte, Ont.)

NC1429.W573A4 2004   741.5'973   C2004-904423-0

Printed in Canada
#1-8-04

Publisher's Note

James Robert Williams was born in Nova Scotia in 1888 and his family moved to Detroit before he started school. At age 15 he quit school to apprentice as a machinist, moving to Arkansas and then Oklahoma where he spent six years drifting around the territory working as a cowboy on different ranches before spending three years in the U.S. Cavalry. After he married, he took a full-time job with a crane company in Ohio. He started cartooning professionally in 1922 with the daily cartoon "Out Our Way", drawing heavily on his experiences in the military, in machine shops and on ranches. At the peak of his career "Out Our Way" was carried by some 700 newspapers. He bought his own ranch in 1930 and continued drawing until his death in 1957. His lifetime production was in excess of 10,000 cartoons.

Leonard G. Lee, Publisher
Almonte, Ontario
August 2004

How We Make Our Books - You may not have noticed, but this book is quite different from other softcover books you might own. The vast majority of paperbacks, whether mass-market or the more expensive trade paperbacks, have the pages sheared and notched at the spine so that they may be glued together. The paper itself is often of newsprint quality. Over time, the paper will brown and the spine will crack if flexed. Eventually the pages fall out.

All of our softcover books, like our hardcover books, have sewn bindings. The pages are sewn in signatures of sixteen or thirty-two pages and these signatures are then sewn to each other. They are also glued at the back but the glue is used primarily to hold the cover on, not to hold the pages together.

We also use only acid-free paper in our books. This paper does not yellow over time. A century from now, this book will have paper of its original color and an intact binding, unless it has been exposed to fire, water, or other catastrophe.

There is one more thing you will note about this book as you read it; it opens easily and does not require constant hand pressure to keep it open. In all but the smallest sizes, all our books will also lie open on a table, something that a book bound only with glue will never do unless you have broken its spine.

The cost of these extras is well below their value and while we do not expect a medal for incorporating them, we did want you to notice them.

U.S. CAVALRY CARTOONS

J.R. WILLIAMS

Algrove Publishing
Classic Reprint Series

THE STOP LIGHTS

1

MOMENTS WE'D LIKE TO LIVE OVER
REVEILLE.

THE DRY WORKER.

WAR COLLEGE.

J.R.WILLIAMS

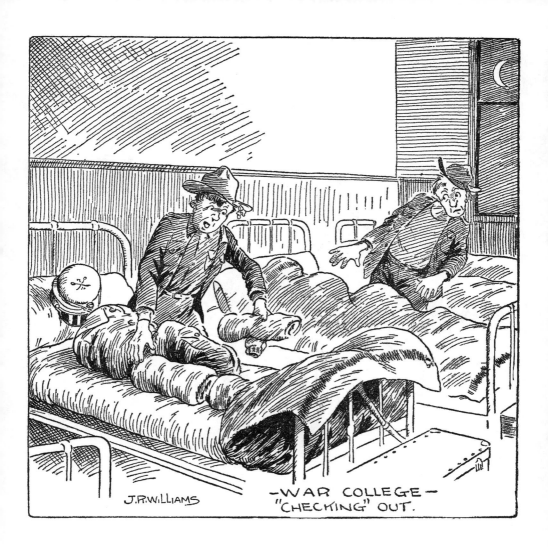

—WAR COLLEGE—
"CHECKING" OUT.

J.P.WILLIAMS

- WAR COLLEGE -
THE DIPLOMA

J.P. WILLIAMS

10

DOUBLE EXPOSURE.

J.P.Williams

WAR COLLEGE.

13

THE NEUTRALS AND THE WARRIOR.

THE SURPRISE PACKAGE.

WAR COLLEGE

16

WAR COLLEGE — "SLOW MUSIC."

INSPECTION ARMS."

J.P.WILLIAMS

-WAR COLLEGE-
THE OUTSIDER.

19

THE GROOM AND THE "FOOT MEN"

J.R.WILLIAMS

"THE HEADLESS HORSEMAN."

THE GERM CARRIER.

J.P.WILLIAMS

THE TIP.

J.P.WILLIAMS

-WAR COLLEGE-
THE "DOG ROBBER."

THE UNEMPLOYMENT OFFICE   J.P.WiLLiAMS

25

THE GUARD AND THE GUARDIANS · J.R.WILLIAMS

27

WAR COLLEGE ~ THE STIFF.

J.R.WILLIAMS

War College —
Snubbed

J.R.Williams

29

- WAR COLLEGE -
THE SIR CUSS.

J.R.WILLIAMS

30

"GRASS WIDOWS"   J.P.WILLIAMS

WAR COLLEGE — THE "RAIDER"

J.R.WILLIAMS

-WAR COLLEGE-
"SCOUTS OUT."

- WAR COLLEGE -

A NAME OF LONG STANDING

WAR COLLEGE —
THE TWO TIMERS

J.P.WILLIAMS

~WAR COLLEGE~ AN UNFIT SUBJECT.

THE BALL AND CHAIN

J.P.WiLLiAMS

THE EMPLOYMENT · BUREAU

J.P.WILLIAMS

42

"BUTTING" IN.

J.R.WILLIAMS

WAR COLLEGE — SKINNING OUT.

J.R.WILLIAMS

45

HEROES ARE MADE – NOT BORN.

J.P.WILLIAMS

THE UP-SET

J.P.WILLIAMS

"WAR COLLEGE"

SECURITY.

J.R.WILLIAMS

48

THE COME BACK

J.R.WILLIAMS

THE ART CRITICS

J.P. WILLIAMS

50

MARKED MEN.

51

THE "SNIPER."

J.R.WILLIAMS

HEROES ARE MADE — NOT BORN.

J.P.WILLIAMS

THE NON STRADDLER

J.P. WILLIAMS

54

THE LABOR SAVER.

J.P.WILLIAMS

HELPLESS.

J.P.WILLIAMS

"DEALIN' 'EM OFF THE ARM."

J.P.WILLIAMS

"THEM AS HAS GITS."

J.R.WILLIAMS

THE SPELL DOWN.

WRAPPED IN YOUR ARMS.

J.R.WILLIAMS

ADVANCE RESERVATIONS.

THE ALIAS.

J.P.WILLIAMS

THE TRAVELOG.

J.P.WILLIAMS

THE RAIN MAKERS.

J.R.WILLIAMS

ARMED INTERFERENCE.

66

"FINDERS KEEPERS"

J.R.WILLIAMS

"THE LINE'S BUSY"

J.P.Williams

THE ADVANCE ACCOMODATION.

HEROES ARE MADE — NOT BORN.

THE DEAD LETTER.

J.R.WILLIAMS

LOVERS LANE

73

THE WARRIOR.

J.R.WILLIAMS

74

THE DOUBLE STANDARD

THE LONG AND SHORT OF IT.   J.R.WILLIAMS

THE NON-FOLLOWING FOLLOWERS

J.P.WiLLIAMS

COURT MARTIAL AND CURT MARTIAL.

HEROES ARE MADE—NOT BORN

THE GUARD.

J.R.WILLIAMS

80

HEROES ARE MADE - NOT BORN

BORN THIRTY YEARS TOO SOON

BORN THIRTY YEARS TOO SOON

J.R.WILLIAMS

BORN THIRTY YEARS TOO SOON — J.R.WILLIAMS

BORN THIRTY YEARS TOO SOON

BORN THIRTY YEARS TOO SOON

THE INFERIOR SUPERIOR

J.R.WILLIAMS

DEMOCRACY

J.P.WILLIAMS

BORN THIRTY YEARS TOO SOON

BORN THIRTY YEARS TOO SOON   J.R.WILLIAMS

BORN THIRTY YEARS TOO SOON

J.R.WILLIAMS

BORN THIRTY YEARS TOO SOON

J.P.WiLLiAMS

BORN THIRTY YEARS TOO SOON

THE MARTIAL AIR

A HOUSEHOLD NECESSITY

100

BORN THIRTY YEARS TOO SOON

BORN THIRTY YEARS TOO SOON

BORN THIRTY YEARS TOO SOON

J.R.WILLIAMS

BORN THIRTY YEARS TOO SOON

BORN THIRTY YEARS TOO SOON

Lake Forest was and is a well-to-do suburb north of Chicago.

BORN THIRTY YEARS TOO SOON

"SHOES ARE NEXT, SUGAR"!

J.R. WILLIAMS

BORN THIRTY YEARS TOO SOON

J.R.WiLLiAMS

BORN THIRTY YEARS TOO SOON

BORN THIRTY YEARS TOO SOON — J.R.WILLIAMS

BORN THIRTY YEARS TOO SOON

114

BORN THIRTY YEARS TOO SOON

BORN THIRTY YEARS TOO SOON   J.R.WILLIAMS

119

BORN THIRTY YEARS TOO SOON   J.R.WILLIAMS

BORN THIRTY YEARS TOO SOON

BORN THIRTY YEARS TOO SOON

BORN THIRTY YEARS TOO SOON

BORN THIRTY YEARS TOO SOON   J.R.WILLIAMS

BORN THIRTY YEARS TOO SOON

If you are a fan of J.R. Williams, you may be
interested in our other Williams Classic Reprints.

Classic Cowboy Cartoons

The Bull of the Woods

Publications by Algrove Publishing Limited

The following is a list of titles from our popular *"Classic Reprint Series"* as well as a list of other publications by *Algrove Publishing Limited.*

Classic Reprint Series

Other Algrove Publications

Algrove Publishing Limited
36 Mill Street, P.O. Box 1238, Almonte, Ontario, Canada K0A 1A0
Telephone: (613) 256-0350   Fax: (613) 256-0360   Email: sales@algrove.com